Look here!

Sally Hewitt

QED Publishing

QED

A Catalogue record for this book is available
from the British Library.

ISBN 1 84538 167 X

Written by Sally Hewitt
Series Consultant Sally Morgan

Project Editor Honor Head
Series Designer Zeta Jones
Photographer Michael Wicks
Picture Researcher Nic Dean

Publisher Steve Evans
Creative Director Louise Morley
Editorial Manager Jean Coppendale

Printed and bound in China

Picture credits

Alamy Paul Doyle 18/Elizabeth Whiting &
Associates 19
Corbis Ariel Skelley 5/Ralph A. Clevenger
6/ Christoph Wilhelm 7/Gabe Palmer 8, 18/
Roger Ressmeyer 10/Roy Morsch 17
Getty Images E. Dygas/Taxi 5/Jeffrey
Sylvester/Taxi 10/SteveCole/Photographer's
Choice 14/Michael Denora/The Image Bank
16/David Hume Kennerly/Reportage 16/UHB
Trust/Stone 17

The words in bold
like this are
explained in the
Glossary on page 22.

Contents

See this!

You have five senses that give you all kinds of information about what is going on around you.

The five senses are sight, touch, taste, smell and hearing. This book is about sight.

Your sense of sight helps you to see colours and shapes around you and things that move.

Look around you.
What can you see?
What is moving?

▲ Your sight helps you
to cross the road safely.

What colours
can you see?
What colours
do you like
to wear?

▶ When you go
shopping, you
look for things
you like.

How you see

Eyes are the part of your body that you see with.

▸ When your eyes are shut, **light** can't get in and you can't see.

The coloured circle in your eye is the **iris**.

iris

pupil

The black circle in the iris is called the **pupil**. Pupils are holes that let light into your eyes.

When it is dark, your pupils open to let in light. Your pupils get smaller when it is very bright to stop too much light hurting your eyes.

To see your pupils change size, close your eyes for a minute then open them and look in a mirror. Your pupils look big.

Look out of the window in daylight, then look in a mirror. Your pupils should look smaller!

Look and learn

You can learn all kinds of things when you look carefully.

Look at these children. Can you tell if they are happy or sad?
Can you tell where they are going?

What else can you tell about them just by looking?

Your eyes send messages to your brain
about what you see.

Look carefully at these pictures then
cover them up. What can you remember?

ball
plate
flower
rubber duck

How many things are there?
What colour is the ball?
What colour is the flower?
What else can you remember?

9

Two eyes

You have two eyes in the front of your head. The **eyeballs** in your eyes move together. They can move up and down, and left and right.

◀ You have to turn your head around to see what is going on behind you.

▶ A chameleon can look up with one eye and down with the other eye at the same time!

10

Your two eyes help you to tell how far away something is. It is harder to tell with one eye shut.

- Hold your arms out in front of you.
- Put a top on a pen.
- Now try and put the top on the pen with one eye shut.

How easy is it with one eye shut?

11

How your eyes work

When you look at something, a picture of it is made on the back of your eyes. This picture is upside down!

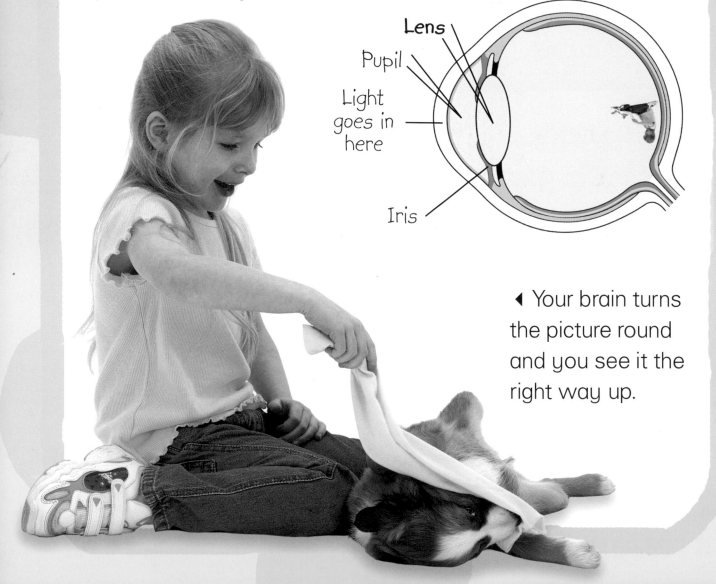

Lens

Pupil

Light goes in here

Iris

◀ Your brain turns the picture round and you see it the right way up.

Your eyes can see colours
clearly in bright light.

What colours
can you see in
this picture?

In the dark,
most colours
look grey.

▶ In the dark, you
might see the shapes of
this picture, but the colours
would look grey.

Bigger and smaller

Lenses are curved pieces of glass or plastic. They make things look bigger, smaller, nearer or further away.

Lenses in a telescope make things look nearer.

◀ A planet looks like a dot in the night sky. A telescope makes it bigger.

14

A **magnifying glass** makes things look bigger. The lens is curved and is thicker in the middle.

◄ You can see the pattern of your fingerprint under a magnifying glass lens.

Activity

These are objects that have been magnified. Can you tell what they are?

▶ This is a juicy fruit.

◄ You might use this for your hair.

Wearing glasses

The lenses used in glasses help people to see things more clearly.

◀ Long-sighted people need glasses to help them to read and to see things close up.

▶ Short-sighted people need glasses to see things in the distance.

◀ Contact lenses
work in the same
way as glasses,
but the lens is
put straight onto
the eye.

Sunglasses have dark
lenses. These lenses
help to protect
your eyes in
bright sunlight.

17

Being blind

People who are blind learn to use their other senses to give them information.

The sound of someone's voice tells them how that person is feeling.

◀ Blind children use their sense of touch to learn.

▶ Blind children can learn to read by feeling raised dots called Braille.

Blind people can find things if they are always kept in the same place.

Why should a room be kept tidy for someone who can't see?

▶ This tidy bedroom belongs to someone who can't see. Toys left lying on the floor could be dangerous.

Trick your eyes

Your eyes can be tricked into seeing things that aren't really there.

◄ Look at this picture. Do you see a rabbit or a duck? Or both?

Optical illusions are pictures that look like one thing, but could be another. Like the picture on this page.

A film looks like one long moving picture, but it is lots of still pictures shown one after the other very fast.

Activity

Make your own moving film!

- Draw 5 pictures like these:

- Put the pages in order like this and flick them quickly to see the figure run.

Glossary

Eyeballs

Your eyes are shaped like small, round balls. You can see only the front part of your eyeballs.

Iris

The coloured part of your eye is called the iris. People have different coloured irises such as green, blue and brown.

Lens

The lens in your eye helps you to see things. Lenses in glasses or binoculars make things look bigger or smaller.

Light

Light comes from the Sun or electric lights or fire. Your pupils get larger or smaller to let in, or keep out, light.

Magnifying glass

A magnifying glass has a curved glass or plastic lens. It makes things look bigger.

Pupil

The black circle in your eye is called the pupil. Your pupils are holes which open and close to let in light or keep out light.

Index

Parents' and teachers' notes

- Divide the class into pairs. Ask the children to identify the pupils and irises in each others' eyes. Guess which is the most common eye colour in the class. Make a block graph recording the children's eye colours and compare the result with the children's guesses.

- Play games that involve looking carefully. Show the children a picture then take it away and ask them questions about it. What have they remembered? *I-Spy* and *Pairs* are good games for looking and remembering.

- Collect things that children can discuss. For example, a page from a children's clothes catalogue, well-known paintings, flowers or pieces of material. Ask the children to describe them. Talk about what they like or dislike about the look of them, such as the colour or the shape.

- Talk about protecting your eyes. Never look directly at the Sun. Sunglasses help to protect your eyes from bright sunlight. Goggles help to protect your eyes in a swimming pool.

- Look at pictures of animals and talk about their eyes. Are they on the front or the sides of their heads? Are their eyes big or small? Do the animals have to see at night or underwater? Do they use their eyes for hunting?

- Explain that we see things when light from them goes into our eyes. Try looking at a bunch of flowers in bright light, in shadow, and then in a darkened room. Talk about how the amount of light changes what you can see.